THE SEEKER'S WORKBOOK

The Seeker's

Workbook

PRACTICES FOR HEALING, INTEGRATION, AND BECOMING

Rowena Sowders

QUIET CUP
PRESS

Copyright

For the Seeker.

Whoever you are,

when you open this book,

you are allowed to be here.

Contents

Before You Begin

A note on truth, tenderness, and doing this on your terms.

This workbook is not here to fix you. You are not a broken thing.

It is here to help you listen to yourself, the way you might listen to a friend you love, with honesty, patience, and enough softness to make the truth feel safe to touch.

Some parts of this work will feel easy. Some parts might tighten your chest a little. If that happens, pause.

Put your feet on the floor.

Take a breath.

Drink some water.

Look around the room and name five things you can see.

You are allowed to regulate.
You are allowed to take breaks.
You are allowed to go slow.

You don't have to do this perfectly. There is no gold star for suffering through it.

What matters is that you show up as you are, and you keep choosing yourself, one page at a time.

A Note on Memory

On gaps, fragments, and what your body still knows.

You may not remember everything.

You may remember in flashes, sensations, and sudden emotional weather that rolls in without warning. You may remember through dreams, through body cues, through a sentence in this workbook that lands like a bell in your ribs.

That counts.

Memory is not always linear. Healing isn't either.

If you have blanks, you are not doing it wrong. If your story comes in pieces, you are not failing. You are human. You are protected. You are unfolding.

Let what rises be enough for today.

How to Use This Workbook

A gentle structure for brave work.
Each module follows the same rhythm, so you can relax into the process.

The Wound
What shaped you, what hurt, what still pulls at the thread.

The Lesson
What you learned, what you survived, what you began to understand.

The Becoming
What is changing now, what you are growing into, what you are ready to live differently.

Inside each module you'll find:

- Reflective Journaling Prompts

- Embodiment practices (simple, grounded, and realistic)

- Creative invitations (because truth does not always arrive in paragraphs)

- A short soul note from me to you

- A breath interlude to help you transition and come back to your body

You do not have to complete every prompt. Choose the ones that speak to you. Skip what doesn't. Return later if you want. Your pace is part of the work

You may also find yourself returning to this workbook more than once.

Not because you missed something the first time, but because healing often unfolds in layers. When one truth settles, it creates space for another to emerge. What once felt unreachable may become accessible later, when your system feels safer or more resourced.

The pages don't change. You do.

Each return is a sign that something new in you is ready to be met.

About the Breath-Poem Interludes

Box breathing made lyrical.

Between modules, you'll find short breath-poems paced to box breathing.

Box breathing is straightforward:
inhale to the count of four, hold for four, exhale for four, hold for four.

These interludes are not performance. They are not spiritual gatekeeping. They are a pause, a reset, a way to help your nervous system stay with you while you do deeper reflection.

When you see breath cues, try one round. If you want to do more, do more. If you hate breathwork, congratulations, you're still allowed to use this workbook. Skip it and keep going.

Here is what the format looks like:

(inhale)
a line to enter your body

(hold)
a line to steady

(exhale)
a line to soften or release

(hold)
a line to make room for what comes next

Each module will have its own breath-poem, and at the end of the workbook you'll find a full collection of them in one place, so you can return to them anytime.

Welcome, Seeker

This is not just my story; it's a mirror for yours.

This workbook was born from a simple truth: healing becomes possible when we stop abandoning ourselves.

You don't need a perfectly organized past to do this work.
You don't need a tidy timeline.
You don't need permission from anyone who benefited from your silence.

You only need a willingness to be honest, and a willingness to be gentle.

This is a working book.
It is meant to be written in. Scribbled through. Doodled on. Bent at the corners. Lived with.

You'll notice a lot of white space throughout these pages. That isn't emptiness. It is an invitation.

Some pages hold more space than words on purpose. That space is not there to test you, rush you, or make you feel awkward. It isn't silence as punishment or neglect.
It is room.

For some people, space feels calming. For others, it can stir restlessness, questions, old fears. If your mind starts racing, wondering if you missed something, did something wrong, or are supposed to be filling the silence, pause. Nothing is wrong. You didn't fail the page. The page is doing its job.

That space is where your thoughts get louder.
Where feelings have room to move.
Where something you've been carrying finally has permission to show itself. Put it there.

Use the margins. Write sideways if you want.
Circle words that hum. Cross out what doesn't fit.
Sketch shapes instead of sentences. Let your thoughts spill wherever they land.

There is no "right" way to move through this book. There is only your way.

If you're a "keeping the pages clean" kind of person (I get it), keep a notebook nearby. The method doesn't matter. What matters is that your truth has somewhere to land.

If the page ever feels too small, that's okay. Grab another notebook, a scrap of paper, the back of an envelope. What matters isn't where the words go, but that they make their way out of your body and into the world.

This is your workbook.
Your safe place.
You are allowed to feel what rises here.
You are allowed to think the thoughts you've been pushing away.
You are allowed to learn from what shows up.

There is no finish line here.
Just a beginning.
A pause.
A breath.
A return.

This workbook can hold it
And so can you.

Part I: Foundations

The Blueprint Beneath Me

Core Theme

Before we had words, we had roots.

This module explores the early imprints that shaped who we believed we had to be in order to survive, belong, or stay safe. It looks at the emotional architecture laid down in childhood, the roles we stepped into without consent, and the quiet strengths that formed alongside the wounds.

This is not about assigning blame. It is about understanding the foundation you were built on, so you can decide what still supports you and what no longer needs to hold the weight of your life.

Before you write anything.

Pause here for a moment.

Can you think of a time early in your life when you learned something about who you needed to be in order to feel safe, accepted, or loved?

You don't need a clear memory. An image, a feeling, or even a body sensation is enough.

There is no need to analyze this yet. Just notice what rises.

The Wound

Some of our earliest lessons were learned before memory could organize them.

Many of us grew up sensing the emotional weather of our homes, learning to read moods, anticipate needs, and adjust ourselves accordingly. Safety may not have felt like something we could assume. Instead, we learned to create it through vigilance, usefulness, quietness or strength.

The wound here is not a single event. It is the slow shaping of the nervous system. The belief that love or stability required effort. The feeling that rest, softness, or space had to be earned.

Pause here for a moment.

As you read these words, notice which ones feel familiar. You may recognize them in how you move through the world now, how you respond to stress, or how you relate to rest and closeness.

You don't need to tell the whole story. You might begin by finishing one sentence:

I learned early that I needed to be...

Write only what feels accessible today.

The Lesson

Even in those early years, something in you knew.

Alongside the adaptation lived intuition.
Alongside the bracing lived awareness.
Alongside the responsibility lived resilience.

You learned how to endure, yes, but you also learned how to listen.
You learned how to feel deeply.
You learned how to hold complexity long before you had language for it.

The lesson is this: What helped you survive was not weakness. It was intelligence. It was wisdom responding to its environment.

Pause here for a moment.

Take a moment to consider how this intelligence has shown up in your life. If it feels right, write about one way this intelligence protected you.

You are not being asked to justify the cost of it, only to acknowledge its purpose. Nothing you did to survive was accidental.

The Becoming

Foundations are not destinies.

What was built early can be examined, adjusted, and reshaped. You are no longer that small body absorbing everything without choice. You have the capacity now to decide which roots nourish you and which ones are ready to be loosened.

Becoming begins with curiosity. With compassion for who you were. With permission to build something new on the bones of what already exists.

You are allowed to redesign the structure of your life without erasing where you came from.

Pause here for a moment.

Take a moment to reflect on what feels ready to change.

As you write, you might notice:

- Something that has supported you but no longer fits.
- Something that still feels steady and worth keeping.

There is no need to decide everything at once. Begin wherever your attention naturally goes.

Reflective Journaling Prompts

Take these slowly. You do not need to answer them all at once.

- What emotional roles did you take on early in life, even if no one explicitly asked you to?

- How did you learn to stay safe as a child? Through quietness, caretaking, achievement, vigilance, humor, or something else?

- What beliefs about love, safety, or belonging did you absorb before you had words for them?

- Which of those beliefs still influence your choices today?

- What part of you learned strength alongside survival? How does that strength show up now?

Let your answers be incomplete. Let them arrive in fragments if they need to.

Use the pages that follow in your own way, slowly or not at all.

Embodiment Practice

Establishing Ground

This practice helps orient your body to the present, reminding it that you are here, now, and no longer required to brace.

Sit with your feet flat on the floor.
Press them gently down and notice the sensation.
Place one hand on your chest and one on your lower belly.

Take five slow breaths.
Notice where your body tightens automatically.
Without forcing change, simply name it.

Silently say:
"I am here."
"I am safe enough in this moment."
"My body does not need to carry everything alone."

If emotion rises, let it. If nothing rises, that is fine too.

Creative Invitation

Mapping Your Roots

Draw a simple shape that represents you.
From it, sketch lines outward like roots.

Along each root, write or draw early influences.
Roles. Messages. Family patterns. Unspoken rules.
Do not analyze yet. Just notice.

Then circle the roots that still nourish you.
Cross lightly through the ones that feel heavy or outdated.

This is not erasure.
It is discernment.

A Soul Note from Me to You

You were not too much.

You were too aware in a world that needed your quiet competence.

You learned to notice, to adapt, to carry what others could not.

That wasn't a flaw. That was survival shaped into skill.

The parts of you that learned early were doing their best with what they had.

They kept you safe. They kept you moving.

You do not need to dismantle them with anger.

You can thank them.

You can walk with them.

And you can gently set boundaries with them now.

Nothing about your foundation was accidental.

Every way you learned to be had a reason.

But you are no longer required to live inside its original blueprint.

I'm here with you as you look at it.

You don't have to rush. You don't have to get it right.

We can take this one step at a time.

You get to revise.

Breath-Poem Interlude I

Grounding

(inhale)
Feel the floor beneath you

(hold)
Let your body arrive

(exhale)
Release what does not belong to this moment

(hold)
Rest here, rooted and present

Repeat as needed before moving on.

Your Turn to Speak

Use this space in whatever way feels right.
Words. Lists. Shapes. Arrows. Silence.

And if this page feels too small, that's okay.
Your truth has never fit neatly inside margins.

Part II: Shadows & Survival

Child of the Storm – Through the Shadow Years

Core Theme

Sometimes, the darkness is not a place to escape, but the womb of your becoming.

This module explores the years when safety was inconsistent, truth was complicated, and silence did its own kind of damage. These pages are not here to make you relive anything. They are here to help you notice what those seasons shaped in you, what they taught you to carry, and what you are allowed to set down now.

Take this slowly.
Pause often.
If your body wants a break, that is wisdom, not resistance.

Pause here for a moment.

Before you continue, notice how your body feels right now.
You might place a hand somewhere that feels steady, or take one slow breath.
You are allowed to move at the pace your body sets.

There is no rush.

The Wound

Some storms don't arrive with thunder.
They arrive as tension. As scanning. As bracing. As learning how to survive the mood in a room.

This wound isn't one moment. It's the long shaping of a nervous system that learned:

- love could change without warning

- safety had conditions

- silence could bruise

- responsibility could become identity

When you grow up inside instability, hypervigilance can start to feel like "personality." Control can start to feel like "maturity." Being the strong one can start to feel like the only way to be allowed to exist.

Pause here for a moment.

As you read these patterns, notice which ones feel familiar in your body or in your daily life now. You are not being asked to change them yet; you are being asked to recognize them.

If it feels safe to do so, write about one way this wound shaped how you learned to show up in the world.

The Lesson

Even inside the storm, something in you adapted with intelligence.

You learned pattern-recognition.
You learned how to read the unsaid.
You learned how to keep moving when clarity wasn't available.

And here is the part that matters now: what helped you survive is not the same thing that must lead your life forever.

The lesson is not, "I should have been stronger."
The lesson is, "I was already strong, and now I get to choose something softer."

Pause here for a moment.

Notice what it feels like to imagine choosing softness, even briefly. You don't need to know what that looks like yet.

If it feels right, write about what "softer" might mean for you right now.

The Becoming

You are not only what you endured.

You are also:

- the one who kept going

- the one who told the truth anyway

- the one who protected what mattered

- the one who kept a spark alive in ash

Becoming doesn't always look like a breakthrough. Sometimes it looks like a quiet return to yourself. A decision to stop disappearing. A willingness to live where you once only survived.

Pause here for a moment.

As you sit with these words, notice which one feels most true for you right now.

If it feels right, write about what returning to yourself looks like in this season of your life.

Reflective Journaling Prompts

Choose one. Circle it. Start messy.
If you feel up to it, you may choose another.

- What storms shaped you, not only by what they destroyed, but by what they revealed?

- What did you learn to carry that was never yours to hold?

- Which survival role did you live in most: caretaker, peacekeeper, overachiever, invisible one, truth-teller, watcher? What did it cost you?

- Where does your body still speak the language of those years (jaw, shoulders, breath, sleep, stomach, vigilance)?

- What would safety look like now, if you were allowed to define it?

Let the answers be incomplete.
Let them come in fragments.

Use the pages that follow in your own way, slowly or not at all.

Embodiment Practice

Unbracing the Body (2 minutes)

Sit with both feet on the floor.
Notice what you are holding.

Unclench your jaw.
Let your shoulders drop one small inch.
Let your tongue rest.

Place one hand on your chest and one on your belly.

Inhale for four.
Hold for four.
Exhale for four.
Hold for four.

Repeat three times.

Then ask, gently:
"What am I bracing for?"

You do not have to answer. Just notice.

Creative Invitation

Map Your Storm Language

Draw a simple weather map.
Think of it as a way to show how you learned to move through emotional weather.

Label a few places:

- **Warnings I learned to read**

- **Things I wasn't allowed to say**

- **Safe places I created**

- **The role I played**

- **What I needed**

You can use words, symbols, arrows, scribbles, shapes.
No art skills required. Just honesty.

A Soul Note From Me to You

If you grew up in storms, you may still feel guilty when life is calm.
You may still brace when things are good, waiting for the shift, the drop, the moment it all changes.

That doesn't mean you're broken.
It means your body is loyal to what it learned.
It learned that vigilance kept you safe. It learned that calm could be temporary.

I want you to know this, gently.
You are not doing anything wrong when your body prepares for impact.
It is doing what it once had to do.

And you are allowed to outgrow the strategies that saved you.
You are allowed to let "being strong" mean something different now.
Strong can mean resting.
Strong can mean trusting a good moment enough to stay in it.

You are allowed to live without waiting for the next crash.
I'm here with you as you practice that.
Slowly. Carefully. One calm moment at a time.

Breath-Poem Interlude II

Safety

(inhale)
Notice that you are here.
(hold)
Let yourself be allowed.
(exhale)
Soften what you can in this moment.
(hold)
Release what was never yours to carry.

Repeat as needed.

Your Turn to Speak

Words. Sketches. Lists. Scribbles.
Let it out of your body and onto paper.

Part III: Voice & Emergence

What the Silence Held

Core Theme

Your voice is the echo of everything you've survived and everything you still believe is possible.

Silence is never empty. It carries memory, protection, fear, and sometimes, survival. This module explores the years when your voice began to return, not as noise, but as truth. Not as performance, but as presence.

Move slowly here. Speaking after silence can feel vulnerable, even when it is long overdue.

Pause here for a moment.

You don't need to say everything at once.

The Wound

Silence was not chosen freely.

It was learned. Practiced. Reinforced.
It kept you safe when speaking carried consequences.
It taught your body when to shrink, when to wait, when to hold everything inside.

Over time, silence can begin to feel like identity rather than strategy.

Pause here for a moment.

As you read this, notice where silence still shows up in your body or your daily life.

You are not being asked to break it yet. You are being asked to understand it.

The Lesson

Your voice never disappeared.

It adapted. It whispered. It hid in notebooks, dreams, questions, and late-night thoughts. It waited for conditions that felt safer. It waited for *you* to be ready.

The lesson here is not "I should have spoken sooner."
The lesson is, "I spoke when I could."

Pause here for a moment.

Notice what it feels like to read that sentence with kindness instead of judgment. You don't need to rewrite the past to honor the timing that protected you.

The Becoming

Voice returns in stages.

First, in truth you admit to yourself.
Then, in boundaries you speak aloud.
Then, in choices that honor what you know.

Speaking becomes less about being heard and more about being whole.

Pause here for a moment.

As you read this, notice which stage feels most present for you right now. You don't need to move ahead of yourself.

Reflective Journaling Prompts

Choose what calls to you. Skip what doesn't.

- What truths did you once silence in order to belong or stay safe?

- How did your voice find expression anyway (writing, dreaming, caretaking, studying, leaving)?

- Where does your body still brace before speaking?

- What feels safer now than it once did?

Use the pages that follow in your own way, slowly or not at all.

Embodiment Practice

Finding Voice Without Sound

Place one hand on your throat, one on your chest.

Breathe slowly.

Without speaking, notice:
Where does your voice live in your body right now?

No fixing. Just noticing.

Creative Invitation

Write What Was Never Said

Begin a sentence and don't plan the ending.

"I never said…"

Let it go where it needs to go.

A Soul Note From Me to You

Your voice does not need to justify itself.

It does not need to persuade, convince, or perform.
It only needs to exist.

There may be moments when your voice feels small, unsteady, or unsure.
That does not make it less true.
It makes it human.

You are allowed to speak even if your voice shakes.
Especially then.

You do not owe clarity to anyone before you offer honesty.
You do not need to be certain to be sincere.
You do not need permission to name what you know.

Your voice was never meant to be perfect.
It was meant to be yours.

Breath-Poem Interlude III

Voice

(inhale)
Notice the feeling rising in your body.
(hold)
Let yourself trust what you sense.
(exhale)
Speak only when it feels true.
(hold)
Stay with yourself as you are.

Repeat as needed.

Your Turn to Speak

No prompts now.

Just space.

Part IV: Love, Loss & the Body

What the Ache Was Always Saying

Core Theme

To love after loss, to hope after heartbreak, that is the bravest kind of magic.

Love is not only romance. It is attachment, safety, longing, protection, devotion, and the deep wish to be held without having to earn it.

This module explores how the body carries love's ache, and how that ache can become guidance rather than pain.

Pause here for a moment.

As you read this, notice where your body holds tenderness, ache, or memory right now.

You don't need to make meaning of it yet.

The Wound

The ache began before it had language.

It lived in the body as tension, vigilance, longing, and fatigue.
It showed up as the need to protect, to endure, to stay alert.
It learned that love often came with loss, control, or disappearance.

For many of us, love was not sanctuary.
It was something to survive.

Pause here for a moment.

As you read this, notice where your body holds ache, protection, or longing right now. You are not being asked to revisit what hurt. You are being asked to notice what your body learned about love.

The Lesson

The ache was never weakness.

It was information.

It pointed toward what was missing, what was unsafe, and what the body still hoped was possible. It asked again and again: *Will you listen this time?*

Pain was not the enemy. Silence was not the cure.
Listening was the doorway.

Pause here for a moment.

As you read this, notice what your body has been trying to tell you, quietly or loudly, for a long time. You don't have to understand it all at once. I'm here with you as you learn how to listen.

The Becoming

Love began to change shape.

Not as fireworks or rescue, but as steadiness.
Not as control, but as presence.
Not as performance, but as rest.

Safety became something practiced, not promised.
Softness became strength.
The body learned to unclench.

Pause here for a moment.

As you read this, notice what it feels like to imagine love as something steady rather than earned. You don't need to rush this learning. I'm here with you as your body takes this in.

Reflective Journaling Prompts

Move slowly. Let your body answer before your mind does.

- Where does ache live in your body right now?

- What has your body been trying to tell you through pain, fatigue, or tension?

- How did you learn what love was supposed to feel like?

- What does love that feels safe look like, even in its smallest form?

- What would choosing yourself look like today, not dramatically, but quietly?

Use the pages that follow in your own way, slowly or not at all.

Embodiment Practice

Listening to the Ache

Place one hand where you feel tension most often.
Place the other on your heart or belly.

Breathe.

Ask silently: *What are you asking me to notice?*
No fixing. No answering. Just listening.

Creative Invitation

Redefining Love

Complete one or more of these without overthinking:

- Love does not have to be…

- Safety feels like…

- When I imagine rest, my body…

- Softness scares me because…

- What I long for is…

A Soul Note From Me to You

Longing is not a flaw.

It is the soul remembering what it deserves.
It is the quiet knowing that something truer exists, even if you haven't felt it fully yet.

You are not asking for too much.
You are not being unrealistic or demanding or difficult.

You are asking for truth.
For steadiness.
For love that doesn't require you to disappear or diminish yourself.

I want you to hear this gently.
Your longing did not come from nowhere.
It came from a place in you that knows what safety feels like, even if it has been rare.

You don't need to silence that knowing to be loved.
You don't need to settle to be chosen.

I'm here with you as you listen to what your longing has been trying to say.
You don't have to rush what's been waiting.

Breath-Poem Interlude IV

Sanctuary

(inhale)
Allow your body to soften here.
(hold)
Listen without needing to respond.
(exhale)
Let the moment open around you.
(hold)
Remain, supported and present.

Repeat as needed.

Your Turn to Speak

No structure now.

Just space.

Part V: Power & Sovereignty

The Space I Stopped Shrinking In

Core Theme

Power is not force.
It is presence.

It lives in the moments you stop apologizing for your body, your needs, your limits, and your becoming.

This module explores what happens when you stop shrinking and begin inhabiting your life from the inside out.

Pause here for a moment.

As you read this, notice where you still tighten, shrink, or apologize without meaning to.

You are allowed to take up space here.

The Wound

Shrinking became a strategy.

For safety.
For belonging.
For survival.

You learned to carry more than was yours.
To say yes when your body said no.
To mistake endurance for worth.

Your body kept the score.

Pause here for a moment.

As you read this, notice where you still shrink, carry, or push past your own limits without realizing it. You are not being asked to stop yet. You are being asked to see what it cost.

The Lesson

The body does not betray.
It communicates.

Collapse, exhaustion, pain, stillness, and grief are not failures.
They are messages.

Power begins when you listen without judgment and stop negotiating your own limits.

Pause here for a moment.

As you read this, notice what your body has been asking for that you've talked yourself out of. You don't need to justify your limits.

The Becoming

Power softened.

It stopped performing.
It stopped proving.
It learned to rest.

Boundaries became acts of devotion.
Stillness became sacred.
Choice became embodied.

You did not disappear when you slowed down.
You arrived.

Pause here for a moment.

As you read this, notice what it feels like in your body to imagine power that rests instead of performs. You don't need to prove your presence to keep it.

Reflective Journaling Prompts

Answer from your body, not from the version of the story you learned to tell.

- Where in your life have you learned to shrink in order to belong?

- What signals has your body used to ask for rest, space, or protection?

- When have you mistaken endurance for strength?

- What does power feel like in your body when it is quiet rather than forceful?

- Where might you practice taking up space without explanation?

Use the pages that follow in your own way, slowly or not at all.

Embodiment Practice

Taking Up Space

Sit or stand and notice your posture.
Without forcing anything, allow your spine to lengthen.
Let your shoulders drop.
Let your breath widen.

Say silently: "I am allowed to be here."

Notice what shifts.

Creative Invitation

- Draw the shape of your boundary.

- Write a list of things you no longer carry.

- Complete the sentence: *Power, for me, looks like…*

A Soul Note From Me to You

I learned that power does not come from staying upright at all costs. It comes from listening when the body says "enough" and believing it.

For a long time, I thought strength meant override.
Push through.
Carry on.
I thought rest was something you earned after collapse, not something you were allowed to choose.

But my body kept telling the truth, quietly at first, then more clearly. It was not trying to stop me. It was trying to keep me.

Power changed for me when I stopped arguing with that voice.
When presence began to matter more than endurance, and slowing down no longer felt like disappearance, but arrival.

I'm here with you as you learn what power feels like when it no longer demands proof.
You don't have to hold yourself up alone anymore.

Breath-Poem Interlude

Space

(inhale)

Let yourself arrive fully here.

(hold)

Notice that you are staying.

(exhale)

Soften into this steady moment.

(hold)

Remain without needing to move.

Repeat as needed.

Your Turn to Speak

Unstructured space stays. Absolutely.

This is where the body needs room.

Part VI: Faith & Inner Authority

The Faith I Built in the Dark

Core Theme

Faith didn't come to me as certainty.

It came as endurance.

As breath.

As the quiet decision to stay when everything in me wanted answers that never arrived.

This module isn't about belief systems or spiritual conclusions. It's about trust, the kind built slowly, from lived experience, intuition, grief, and ordinary moments of care. The kind that forms when you stop pretending, you're not asking questions anymore.

Here, faith is not something you prove.

It's something you notice.

Pause here for a moment.

As you read this, notice what faith has looked like for you when certainty wasn't available. You don't need answers to trust what's carried you this far.

The Wound

I learned early that questions were dangerous.
That belief was something you performed correctly or paid for.
That curiosity could cost you safety.

So, I learned to stay quiet.
To nod when I didn't agree.
To fold parts of myself away so I wouldn't be labeled, corrected, or dismissed.

The wound wasn't doubt.
It was silence.

Pause here for a moment.

As you read this, notice where silence once felt safer than curiosity. You are not being asked to speak yet. You are being asked to understand what silence protected.

The Lesson

Faith isn't obedience.
It isn't certainty.
And it isn't something you inherit intact.

What I learned, slowly and sometimes painfully, is that trust can be rebuilt on your own terms. That questioning doesn't mean you've lost your way. Often, it means you're finally listening.

Faith doesn't require you to abandon yourself.
If it does, it isn't faith.

Pause here for a moment.

As you read this, notice what it feels like to imagine trust that includes you instead of erasing you. You are allowed to rebuild faith in a way that lets you stay whole.

The Becoming

What emerged wasn't louder belief, but quieter knowing.

I stopped looking for permission to trust what steadied me.
I stopped measuring the sacred by other people's rules.
I began to notice what stayed when everything else fell away.

Faith became less about answers and more about presence.
Less about certainty and more about honesty.
Less about performance and more about return.

Pause here for a moment.

As you read this, notice what has steadied you when answers weren't available. You don't need certainty to trust what has carried you.

Reflective Journaling Prompts

Move through these gently. You don't need to answer them all. Let the one that stirs something be enough for now.

- What messages about faith, worth, or belonging were handed to you growing up?

- Where did you feel pressure to believe, perform, or stay silent?

- What experiences shaped your sense of the sacred, even if they don't fit traditional definitions?

- When have you felt most connected, grounded, or held, without needing explanation?

- What does trust feel like in your body when it's real?

Use the pages that follow in your own way, slowly or not at all.

Embodiment Practice

Sit somewhere comfortable.
Place one hand on your chest, the other on your belly.

Notice your breath without trying to change it.

Ask yourself quietly:
Where do I feel steadiness right now?

You don't need words. Sensation is enough.
Stay there for a few breaths.

Creative Invitation

Faith doesn't always come through words.

You might want to draw symbols that feel grounding.
Write fragments instead of sentences.
Create a list of moments when something unseen carried you through.

There is no right form here.
Only honesty.

A Soul Note From Me to You

You are not faithless because you ask questions.

You are not broken because belief shifted.

You are not wrong because your truth doesn't fit neatly into someone else's frame.

Questioning is not betrayal.

It is attention.

It is care directed inward instead of performed outward.

For a long time, you may have been taught that silence was reverence.

That staying quiet was humility.

That belonging required agreement.

But the sacred does not require your silence.

It never did.

If something asked you to disappear in order to belong, it was not asking for faith.

It was asking for compliance.

I'm here with you as you learn to trust what still speaks when certainty falls away.

You don't have to abandon yourself to be devoted.

You never did.

Breath-Poem Interlude

Trust

(inhale)
Notice what continues to hold you

(hold)
Let the need for certainty rest

(exhale)
Release what no longer feels supportive

(hold)
Stay with what remains

Repeat as needed.

Your Turn to Speak

Say it your way: words, sketches, fragments, arrows, messy lists.

Let it come out of your body and onto the page.
You don't have to make it pretty.
You just have to make it true.

Faith Reflection

When Faith Stops Asking to Be Proved

Faith didn't arrive all at once for me.
It didn't announce itself.
It didn't settle anything cleanly.

It showed up in quieter ways.
In staying when leaving would have been easier.
In listening when certainty never came.
In choosing presence over explanation.

Somewhere along the way, I stopped asking faith to save me.
And I stopped asking it to make sense.

Instead, I began to notice what remained when everything else fell away.

What steadied my breath.
What softened my body.
What felt trustworthy not because it promised answers, but because it didn't disappear when questions stayed.

That's when faith changed shape.

It stopped being something I defended.
Stopped being something I performed correctly.
Stopped being something other people had to recognize or approve.

It became something lived.

Faith became the moment I trusted my own reflection instead of the mirrors I was handed.
The moment I let my body lead instead of overriding it.
The moment I allowed mystery to exist without trying to solve it.

Nothing collapsed when I did that.
Nothing was taken from me.

What fell away was pressure.
What remained was presence.

If something has shifted for you here, even slightly, let that be enough.
You do not need to define it.
You do not need to explain it.
You do not need to decide what it means long-term.

Faith doesn't require a conclusion.
It asks only for honesty.

And sometimes honesty sounds like this:
I don't know.
But I'm still here.
And I trust what's holding me.

That is not weakness.
That is not failure.

That is faith, lived quietly, in real time.

Stay with that for a moment before moving on.
Nothing else is required.

Take one breath here before turning the page.

Part VII: Integration

The Quiet Practice of Staying

Core Theme

Integration is not the part where you understand everything.
It's the part where understanding stops needing your attention.

This section is not here to add more insight.
It's here to help what you already touched settle into place.

You've listened to wounds.
You've followed the body.
You've allowed voice to return.
You've softened into love, stopped shrinking, and learned to trust without certainty.

Integration is what happens when those experiences stop being moments and start becoming orientation.

Pause here for a moment.

This is not a conclusion.
It's a gathering.

The Seven Pillars of Integration

Think of these not as rules, but as supports.

They are not steps to complete.

They are places you can return to when things feel wobbly.

You may recognize some immediately.

Others may only make sense later.

You don't need to carry all seven at once.

Let them be reference points, not expectations.

1. The Body as First Language

Your body notices before your mind explains.

Tension, ease, fatigue, breath, ache, and relief are information, not inconveniences.

2. Pace Over Performance

Healing does not move faster because you demand it.

It moves when the nervous system feels safe enough to continue.

3. Boundaries as Care

Limits are not punishment.

They are how trust is protected.

4. Rest as Integration

Rest is not a pause from the work.

It is where the work lands.

5. Curiosity Over Certainty

Questions are not failure.

They are often the first sign of trust.

6. Choice Over Compulsion

You are no longer required to repeat what once kept you safe.

Awareness creates options.

7. Return Is Always Available

There is no falling off the path.

Only moments when you notice you've drifted and come back.

You do not need to memorize these.

You only need to notice which one feels most relevant right now.

That is where integration is already happening.

When the Body and Dreams Speak Together

Some understanding never arrives as words.

It arrives as sensation.

As images that repeat.

As dreams that change tone before they change content.

Your body and your dreams have been in conversation long before this workbook entered your life. This section simply gives that conversation permission.

You may notice patterns like:

recurring images in dreams,

familiar sensations during stress or calm,

instinctive movements toward or away from certain situations,

a sense of knowing without explanation.

None of this needs interpretation in the traditional sense.

Instead, try asking:

What is being practiced here?

Sometimes the body rehearses safety.

Sometimes dreams practice choice.

Sometimes both are testing what it feels like to stay present without bracing.

This is not symbolism to decode.

It's communication to respect.

You don't need to make meaning out of everything.

You only need to notice when something feels different than it used to.

That difference is integration.

Integration Maps

Integration is easier when you can see it.

Not as a timeline.
Not as a narrative.
But as a pattern of supports.

On the next pages, you'll find space to create your own integration map.

There is no correct format.

You might map:
what steadies you,
what signals misalignment,
what helps you return,
what drains you now that didn't before,
what feels non-negotiable for your well-being.

You can use:
words, arrows, symbols, shapes, lists, or no language at all.

This is not an artistic exercise.
It's an orientation tool.

The purpose of an integration map is not beauty.
It's recognition and orientation.

When things feel noisy, complicated, or unclear, this map reminds you where you already stand.

Integration Reflection

The Sacred Weaving

Integration is not about tying everything together neatly.
It's about allowing different parts of you to exist in the same moment without conflict.

Your history does not disappear.
Your questions do not vanish.
Your body still remembers.

What changes is the relationship between them.

You no longer need to choose between insight and instinct.
Between rest and responsibility.
Between truth and belonging.

The weaving happens quietly.

In the way you pause before overriding yourself.
In the way you recognize when something costs too much.
In the way you let yourself stop explaining.

You are not healed because nothing hurts.
You are integrated because you know how to stay.

Stay with discomfort without collapsing.
Stay with joy without bracing.
Stay with yourself when old patterns knock.

This is sacred not because it is dramatic, but because it is honest.
And honesty, practiced gently, changes everything.

When you are ready, you will move into the final module.
Not to learn something new.
But to walk forward with what already holds.

Part VIII: Walking Forward

Walking Forward with What Holds

Core Theme

Integration is not about carrying everything forward.
It's about knowing what *carries you*.

This final module is not a conclusion.
It's a threshold.

You've already done the remembering.
You've sat with wounds, listened to the body, followed the return of voice, softened into love, stopped shrinking, and built trust where certainty never lived. What remains now is not more work, but **discernment**.

This is the place where insight becomes companionship.
Where wisdom becomes something you live with, not something you revisit only in quiet rooms.

Pause here for a moment.

As you read this, notice what feels steady enough to carry with you now. You don't have to bring it all.

At the Threshold

There comes a moment in healing when the question changes.

It stops being
What happened to me?
or
What does this mean?

And becomes
What do I trust enough to walk with me now?

Integration lives in that shift.

Not in tying everything into a neat bow, but in noticing which truths feel steady under your feet. Which practices feel supportive instead of demanding. Which understandings soften your body instead of tightening it.

This module is not asking you to look backward again.
It's asking you to notice what remains **when you don't**.

What stayed when the story loosened its grip.
What steadied you without effort.
What you reach for instinctively when something inside you wobbles.

You are not meant to leave this work behind.
But you are also not meant to carry all of it forward.

Some things were here to teach.
Some things were here to witness.
And some things are meant to walk with you into the world.

This module helps you recognize the difference.

Before You Begin

Move slowly here, not because this is fragile, but because it is *real*.

You don't need to solve anything.
You don't need to name everything.
You don't need to feel finished.

Let this be a noticing.
A quiet inventory.
A pause where you ask, without pressure:

What actually holds me now?

That answer may come as a word.
A sensation.
A practice.
A boundary.
A rhythm you've already been living without realizing it had a name.

Whatever rises is enough.

You are not stepping into emptiness.
You are stepping forward **with support already in your hands**.

The Shift

There is a moment in healing that rarely announces itself.

It doesn't arrive with relief or certainty.
It doesn't always feel victorious.
Often, it feels almost ordinary.

The shift happens when the body stops bracing for a question that no longer needs answering.
When the story loosens its grip, not because it was resolved, but because it no longer needs to explain you.

You may not remember exactly when it occurred.
You might only notice it in hindsight; in the way certain patterns no longer hook you the way they once did. In the pause that appears before reaction. In the choice to rest instead of push. In the quiet refusal to abandon yourself again.

This is not the end of your work.
It is the moment the work stops living only on the page.

The shift is where insight becomes instinct.
Where compassion becomes a reflex.
Where the body recognizes safety before the mind has time to argue.

You didn't force this.
You didn't perform it correctly.
You lived your way into it.

And that matters.

This section is not about what hurt you.
It's about what no longer has to.

Take a moment here.
Notice what feels different now, even if you can't name it yet.
Notice what doesn't require as much effort to carry.

That is the shift.

You don't need to explain it.
You only need to recognize it.

What Holds

There is a difference between what *shaped* you
and what *supports* you now.

Some truths were necessary teachers.
Some practices were scaffolding.
Some beliefs kept you upright when nothing else could.

But not everything that helped you survive is meant to come with you.

What holds you now is quieter.

It doesn't demand your vigilance.
It doesn't require you to prove anything.
It doesn't ask you to stay small, sharp, or on alert.

What holds you feels steady in the body.

It might be a rhythm you've fallen into without naming it.
A way you breathe when something inside you tightens.
A boundary that no longer feels like defiance, just clarity.
A practice you return to because it steadies you, not because you "should."

What holds you may not look impressive from the outside.
It may be small. Ordinary. Repetitive.

That's how you know it's real.

This is not about carrying wisdom like a badge.
It's about companionship.
About knowing what you can lean into when things wobble.

Some questions to sit with here, gently, without urgency:

- What do I reach for now when I feel unsettled?

- What steadies me without effort?

- What feels supportive rather than demanding?

- What no longer needs to come with me?

You don't need a complete list.
You don't need to name everything.

Even one answer is enough.

Because what truly holds you does not need your constant attention.
It works quietly, in the background, letting you live.

Stay here as long as you need.

When you're ready, we'll move into **Walking Forward**, not as a plan, but as a way of being with what you've already gathered.

Walking Forward

Not as a plan.
Not as a promise to do better.
Not as a reinvention.

But as a continuation.

You don't leave this work behind when you close the book.
You carry it differently.

Walking forward doesn't mean you won't stumble.
It means you recognize the ground faster.
It means you know how to pause without panicking.
It means you trust that steadiness can be rebuilt, again and again, without drama.

What you're bringing with you isn't a set of answers.
It's a relationship with yourself that knows how to listen.

You may notice this showing up quietly:

- You catch yourself before overriding your body.

- You pause instead of pushing.

- You choose less but choose it more honestly.

- You stop explaining yourself where explanation was never required.

This is not regression.
This is integration.

Walking forward means letting your life become the practice.

Not every day will feel grounded.
Not every choice will feel clear.
But you now know how to return.

You know how to ask, *What's being asked of me right now?*

You know how to notice when something costs too much.

You know how to choose steadiness over urgency.

And when old patterns try to reassert themselves, because they will,

you don't need to fight them.

You can recognize them.

Thank them for what they once protected.

And choose differently.

That is walking forward.

Not perfectly.

Not permanently.

But consciously.

Breath-Poem Interlude VII

Forward

(inhale)
Feel the ground that has been holding you this whole time

(hold)
Notice what stays without effort

(exhale)
Release what no longer needs to come with you

(hold)
Let your body remember how to carry only what is true

Repeat as needed

Integration in Motion

This is not the place where everything gets wrapped in a bow.
It's the place where you decide what you're actually taking with you.

Thresholds are quiet by nature. They don't announce themselves with fireworks. They arrive as a pause between breaths, a moment where you realize you are no longer who you were but not yet finished becoming.

This module is about integration in motion.

Not reflection for reflection's sake.
Not excavation.
Not repair.

It's about practice.

How the work you've done lives in your body when you wake up on an ordinary Tuesday.
How your boundaries hold when no one is watching.
How trust shows up when certainty still isn't available.
How you move forward without abandoning what you've learned about yourself.

You don't need to carry everything from this journey.
Some things were tools, not luggage.
Some truths were season specific.
Some pain taught you what you needed to know and can now be set down.

Walking forward is an act of discernment.

This module invites you to notice:

- what steadies you now,

- what signals your body sends when something is no longer aligned,

- what practices help you return when you drift,

- and what promises you are willing to make to yourself, quietly, without witnesses.

There is no pressure here to "apply" everything perfectly.
Life will do that part on its own.

Your only task is to listen for what holds.

Not what impresses.
Not what performs healing.
Not what looks good on the outside.

What holds when things get real.

This is where the story becomes practice.
This is where insight becomes lived rhythm.
This is where you stop asking, *Am I healed?*
and start asking, *How do I want to live with what I now know?*

Stay slow here.
This threshold doesn't close behind you.
You can step back and forth as needed.

When you're ready, we'll move into the first section of this module, where we begin gathering, not everything, just what belongs with you now.

.

The Wound

Even after deep work, there can be a quiet fear that follows you across the threshold.

The fear isn't that you haven't healed enough.
It's that you might forget yourself again.

Many of us were taught, subtly or explicitly, that insight was fragile. That if we didn't stay vigilant, we'd slip back into old patterns, old pain, old versions of ourselves that learned to survive by disappearing. So even growth can come with tension. Even relief can feel provisional.

The wound here is not failure.
It's mistrust of continuity.

It's the belief that what you've learned only exists inside these pages. That once the structure ends, you're on your own again. That wisdom has to be constantly rehearsed to remain real.

This wound often shows up as:

- over-monitoring yourself for "backsliding,"

- pressure to live the lessons flawlessly,

- guilt when old feelings resurface,

- the sense that ease must be earned again each day.

But healing does not erase your history, and it does not require perfection to remain intact. The nervous system doesn't forget every old pathway overnight. That doesn't mean the work didn't land. It means you're human.

Nothing has been lost.
Nothing needs to be re-proven.

The work didn't disappear when you turned the page. It settled. And sometimes, settling feels unfamiliar because you're used to effort.

This wound asks to be met with reassurance, not discipline. With trust, not scrutiny.

You are not walking away from the work.

You are carrying it differently now.

The Lesson

What stays is not the insight you can quote.
It's the response your body reaches for before your mind catches up.

You don't carry healing as a checklist. You carry it as pattern recognition. As a pause that didn't exist before. As a moment where you choose differently without having to argue yourself into it.

The lesson here is simple, and it's easy to overlook because it doesn't announce itself:

What you've learned lives in you now, even when you're not thinking about it.

It shows up when:

- you notice tension and soften instead of powering through,

- you recognize a familiar dynamic and step back sooner,

- you feel the urge to explain yourself and choose not to,

- you rest without narrating your worth,

- you trust a quiet no without needing evidence.

The work did not make you invulnerable.
It made you responsive.

And responsiveness is more durable than certainty.

You no longer need to carry the entire story with you to stay connected to its wisdom. Some lessons dissolve into instinct. Some truths become background music rather than lyrics you have to sing out loud.

This is how integration works. Not through constant remembering, but through embodied recall. Your body knows when something is off. Your breath tells you when you've gone too far. Your discomfort has become information rather than a verdict.

You didn't lose the work when life resumed.
Life is where the work learned how to live.

The lesson is not "I must do this right."

The lesson is **"I will notice when I need to return."**

And return is always available.

The Becoming

Becoming, here, is not a dramatic reinvention.
It's a series of small agreements you make with yourself and keep.

You don't become by force. You become by repetition. By choosing, again and again, not to abandon the signals that tell you the truth.

What's emerging now isn't a new identity. It's a steadier relationship with yourself.

Becoming looks like:

- checking in before you override your own limits,

- trusting the moment your body tightens as information, not inconvenience,

- letting pauses count as progress,

- choosing repair over self-criticism,

- allowing rest to be part of devotion, not a reward for exhaustion.

This is where the work shifts from excavation to stewardship.

You are no longer trying to uncover who you are. You are tending what you've already found.

And tending does not require intensity. It requires attention.

You will still have days where old patterns whisper. That doesn't mean you've failed. It means the nervous system is testing what's familiar. Each time you respond with presence instead of panic, you reinforce something new.

Becoming is not linear. It spirals. It revisits. It deepens.

But here's what's different now:
You recognize yourself sooner.

You don't disappear as quickly.

You don't doubt your signals as easily.

You don't confuse endurance with worth.

The doorway stays open behind you, but you are no longer standing in it, undecided. You are walking forward with what holds, not because everything is resolved, but because you trust yourself to respond when it isn't.

That is becoming.

Reflective Journaling Prompts

This is not a test.
It's a taking-stock.

You've done the remembering. You've done the reckoning. Now this is about choice, the quiet, daily kind that doesn't announce itself but changes everything over time.

Take these slowly. One is enough.

- What do you trust now that you didn't trust before, in yourself, in your body, in your knowing?

- What feels steadier in you, even if it's subtle or unfinished?

- Which patterns still visit, but no longer run the room?

- What have you learned about how you need to move through the world in order to stay intact?

- What practices, boundaries, or truths do you want to carry forward because they actually hold you?

- What are you no longer willing to sacrifice in the name of keeping things smooth, quiet, or acceptable?

If it helps, complete one or more of these without overthinking:

- "I know myself better now when…"

- "When something feels off, I will…"

- "What I no longer override is…"

- "Staying with myself looks like…"

- "The version of me I am choosing to honor now needs…"

Let this be honest rather than eloquent.
Messy rather than resolved.

You are not writing a conclusion.

You are naming a direction.

Use the pages that follow in your own way, slowly or not at all.

Embodiment Practice

Carrying What Holds

This is not about doing something new.
It's about noticing what is already different.

Stand or sit somewhere you won't be interrupted for a few minutes.

Let your feet touch the floor. Really touch it.
Notice the contact. The pressure. The weight.

Place one hand on your chest.
Place the other somewhere that feels natural today, belly, thigh, heart, shoulder.

Take one slow breath in through your nose.
Let it reach all the way down.
Exhale through your mouth.

Now ask yourself, gently, without searching for the "right" answer:

What helps me stay with myself right now?

Don't answer with words yet.
Let your body respond first.

You might notice:

- a posture that feels more upright

- a place that softens

- an urge to shift, stretch, or settle

- a sense of yes, or no, or not anymore

Follow that impulse.

If you feel steadier standing, stand.
If you feel steadier seated, stay seated.
If you feel steadier moving, move slowly.

Now name it quietly, just for you:

- "This is what support feels like."

- "This is what alignment feels like."

- "This is what staying looks like."

Take one more breath.

Inhale, noticing where you feel most present.
Exhale, letting go of one thing you no longer need to carry forward.

That's it.

No insight required.
No transformation necessary.

Just practice recognizing what holds you.

Creative Invitation

What You Carry Forward

This is not about summarizing your work.
It's about choosing what comes with you.

On a fresh page, don't title it yet.
Leave the top blank for a moment.

Begin anywhere. Use words, fragments, symbols, lists, shapes. There is no order required.

Respond to any of these, or let them blur together:

- One truth I trust now is…

- Something I no longer need to explain is…

- A boundary that feels steady in my body is…

- What grounds me when things get loud is…

- What I return to when I forget myself is…

If writing feels like too much, draw instead.

- A doorway.

- A line.

- A symbol.

- An object you would carry in your pocket if you could only take one thing.

When something feels complete, stop.

Now, and only now, give the page a title.
Not a clever one.
A true one.

Something like:

- "What Holds Me"

- "What I Know Now"

- "What Comes With Me"

- Or whatever name arrives without effort

This page is not for perfection.
It's for remembering.

You don't need to revisit everything you've done.
You only need to recognize what stays.

A Soul Note From Me to You

You don't leave this work behind when you turn the page.

You carry it in quieter ways now.
In how quickly you notice your body tightening.
In how you pause instead of pushing.
In how you recognize the difference between urgency and truth.

You didn't come here to be finished.
You came here to be *oriented*.

If you're wondering whether you did this "right," let me answer plainly:
If something in you softened, even once, you did.

If you noticed yourself choosing honesty over habit, you did.
If you stopped abandoning yourself in a small but meaningful way, you did.

You don't need to keep digging.
You don't need to keep proving how much you understand.

The work now is simpler, and harder in a different way.
It's living from what you already know.

Let the practices fade into the background when they need to.
Let the language become instinct instead of instruction.
Let your life be the place where integration happens.

And if you forget, because everyone does, you know where to return.
To breath.
To body.
To the quiet truth that has learned how to speak clearly now.

You are not stepping out unprepared.
You are stepping out *with yourself*.

That's the difference.

The Crossing

This is not a conclusion.

It's a crossing.

A moment where you pause at the edge of what you've uncovered and notice what you're carrying now. Not the weight you arrived with, but what has stayed. What steadied. What proved itself trustworthy when the digging stopped.

Thresholds are quiet places.

They don't announce themselves with certainty or fireworks. They show up as a subtle shift in posture. A breath that reaches deeper than it used to. A decision that no longer requires an explanation.

You have already done the hardest work. You listened when it would have been easier to distract. You stayed when leaving yourself behind was familiar. You allowed truth to surface without forcing it into shape.

This module is not about reflection for reflection's sake.

It is about practice.

About living from what you now know in small, ordinary, repeatable ways.

You are not meant to carry every insight forward. Some things did their job and can rest.

What comes with you now should feel:

Supportive, not sharp.

Grounded, not heavy.

Alive, not rehearsed.

If the earlier modules asked, *What happened?*

This one asks, *How will I live differently because of it?*

Not dramatically.

Not perfectly.

But honestly.

Here, you begin to trust yourself in motion. To let your body, your breath, your boundaries, and your quiet knowing guide you in real time. To stop waiting for certainty and start recognizing steadiness when it appears.

This is where the work becomes lived instead of written.
Where the story becomes practice.
Where you walk forward carrying only what truly holds.

Take a breath before moving on.
You're not behind.
You're right on time.

Part IX: Optional Depth Work

The Wound, The Lesson, The Becoming

A Tarot-based, Intuitive Reflection Practice

Some stories don't finish when a book ends.

They resurface later, in different seasons, when something familiar tightens in the body or an old question taps quietly at the ribs.

This section is here for those moments.

You do not need tarot experience to use this practice.

You do not need to interpret cards "correctly."

You do not need to be in pain to return here.

This is an optional way to listen when something asks for attention.

Return only when something asks. Leave again when it quiets.

How to Use This Practice

When something feels stirred but unclear, you may wish to draw three cards, one for each position below.

If you don't work with tarot, you can use oracle cards, runes, symbols, objects, or simply imagine each position and write from intuition.

There is no right order.

There is no timeline to follow.

Let this be slow.

You are not searching for answers.

You are listening for relationship.

Nothing here requires you to push past your own signals.

The Wound

What is asking to be seen now?

This card reflects what has been activated.
Not necessarily the original pain, but how it is showing up in this moment.

The wound does not mean something is wrong.
It means something remembers.

You might ask:

- What feels tender, reactive, or familiar right now?

- Where does this live in my body?

- What part of me feels small, tight, or alert?

- What does this wound want me to know, not fix?

Let the image speak before you analyze it.

The Lesson

What has already been learned?

This card reflects what you've gained through experience, whether you named it at the time or not.

The lesson is not moral.
It is not self-improvement.
It is lived knowledge.

You might ask:

- What did this experience teach me about myself?

- What strength, clarity, or discernment came from this?

- What do I know now that I didn't then?

- How has my response changed over time?

Notice what no longer needs proving.

The Becoming

How this wisdom wants to live now?

This card reflects integration in motion.
Not who you must become, but how you are already changing.

Becoming is quiet.
It happens in choices, not declarations.

You might ask:

- What is being asked of me now?

- How does this wisdom want to be lived, not explained?

- What feels steady rather than urgent?

- What would it look like to stay with myself here?

Let this be unfinished. Becoming always is.

Closing Note

You do not need to draw these cards every time something hurts.
You do not need to turn every feeling into meaning.

This practice exists so you remember:
You can return without starting over.
You can listen without reopening old wounds.
You can trust that what matters will speak when it's ready.

The story doesn't need to be relived.
It needs to be related to differently.

That is the work now.

Closing: The Becoming

This is not where everything resolves.
It's where everything learns how to live together.

Becoming is not a final form. It's a practice of staying. Staying with what you know. Staying with what you feel. Staying with yourself when old patterns try to reclaim familiar ground.

You didn't arrive here by force.
You arrived by listening.

Along the way, you learned how to pause instead of push. How to recognize the difference between urgency and truth. How to feel what your body was already saying. How to loosen your grip on what never truly held you.

This closing is not meant to summarize what you've read.
It's meant to help you feel what you're carrying now.

What follows is not instruction.
It's reflection.
Witness.
A gentle taking stock before you step back into your life.

Take your time here.
Nothing is asking you to hurry.

Integration Reflection: The Sacred Weaving

Integration is not about keeping everything.

It's about discernment.
About knowing what belongs together now.

You've walked through memory, silence, ache, faith, and return. You've listened to the body. You've followed the voice back to itself. You've learned how trust forms without certainty and how power softens when it's no longer proving anything.

The sacred weaving happens when these pieces stop competing.

When body, voice, intuition, and rest no longer pull in different directions.
When the nervous system stops bracing long enough to recognize safety.
When insight doesn't live only in reflection, but in response.

This is not a moment of arrival.
It's a moment of alignment.

You don't need to be healed to be whole.
You don't need clarity to be faithful.
You don't need answers to be grounded.

Wholeness isn't the absence of contradiction.
It's the ability to hold complexity without abandoning yourself.

The sacred weaving is already happening when:

- you pause before overriding your body,

- you notice when something costs too much,

- you choose rest without justification,

- you trust a quiet knowing without needing proof.

Nothing here is fragile.
Nothing needs guarding.

What has integrated will continue integrating.
What has settled will move with you.

You are not leaving this work behind.
You are letting it live.

A Final Soul Note From Me to You

Dear Seeker,

If you're reading this, something in you stayed.

Stayed with discomfort.
Stayed with uncertainty.
Stayed with the parts of yourself that once felt too quiet, too much, or too inconvenient to trust.

I want you to know something plainly.

You didn't do this wrong.

If you moved slowly, you did it right.
If you skipped pages, you did it right.
If you felt resistance, fatigue, relief, or nothing at all, you did it right.

This work was never about doing more.
It was about stopping the habit of leaving yourself behind.

I hope you noticed moments where something softened.
Moments where the body exhaled before the mind caught up.
Moments where you chose honesty over performance, even quietly.

That counts.

You don't owe this work perfection.
You don't owe it completion.

If there's one thing I want you to carry with you, it's this:

You are allowed to trust yourself even when the path is unfinished.

You don't need to explain your healing.
You don't need to justify your boundaries.
You don't need to earn rest.

If you forget, because everyone does, return gently.

To breath.

To body.

To the quiet truth that knows how to steady you now.

You were never behind.

You were always becoming.

With care,

With respect,

With faith in your knowing,

Me

What I'm Carrying Forward

This is not a list of achievements.
It's a recognition.

What remains when the noise settles.

You might name it in words.
You might draw it.
You might feel it more than describe it.

Consider this a moment of choosing.

You might ask yourself:

- What feels steadier in me now?

- What no longer needs my energy?

- What do I trust without forcing?

- What practice, boundary, or truth actually holds me?

Leave space here.
Let the page be generous.

What you carry forward does not need to be impressive.
It needs to be real.

When you're done, or when you feel complete enough for today, close the book without ceremony.

Nothing is ending.

You're walking forward now, not empty-handed, but unburdened.

And that is more than enough.

Appendix

A place to return, not a place to work

This appendix exists for reference, not performance.

Nothing here needs to be completed in order, or at all.

These pages gather tools, practices, and frameworks that appear throughout the workbook, so you can revisit them without re-reading the entire journey.

Use what helps.

Ignore what doesn't.

Return when something calls you back.

Appendix A: Breath-Poem Interludes (Complete Collection)

A nervous system pause you can return to anytime

You encountered these throughout the workbook as transitions. Here they are in one place, so you can use them independently, without context or storyline.

Before you begin, a reminder:

Box breathing follows a simple rhythm

inhale for four

hold for four

exhale for four

hold for four

You don't need to count perfectly. Let the lines guide your breath.

Breath-Poem Interlude I

Grounding

(inhale)
Feel the floor beneath you

(hold)
Let your body arrive

(exhale)
Release what does not belong to this moment

(hold)
Rest here, rooted and present

Repeat as needed.

Breath-Poem Interlude II

Safety

(inhale)
Notice that you are here

(hold)
Let yourself be allowed

(exhale)
Soften what you can in this moment

(hold)
Release what was never yours to carry

Repeat as needed.

Breath-Poem Interlude III

Voice

(inhale)
Notice the feeling rising in your body

(hold)
Let yourself trust what you sense

(exhale)
Speak only when it feels true

(hold)
Stay with yourself as you are

Repeat as needed.

Breath-Poem Interlude IV

Sanctuary

(inhale)
Allow your body to soften here

(hold)
Listen without needing to respond

(exhale)
Let the moment open around you

(hold)
Remain, supported and present

Repeat as needed.

Breath-Poem Interlude V

Still Here

(inhale)
Let yourself arrive fully here

(hold)
Notice that you are staying

(exhale)
Soften into this steady moment

(hold)
Remain without needing to move

Repeat as needed.

Breath-Poem Interlude VI

Trust

(inhale)
Notice what continues to hold you

(hold)
Let the need for certainty rest

(exhale)
Release what no longer feels supportive

(hold)
Stay with what remains

Repeat as needed.

Breath-Poem Interlude VII

Forward

(inhale)
Feel the ground meeting you

(hold)
Notice what steadies you

(exhale)
Carry only what belongs with you

(hold)
Step forward without rushing

Repeat as needed.

Appendix B: The Seven Pillars of Integration

A reference framework, not a checklist

These pillars are not goals to achieve. They are orienting principles. You may notice one growing stronger in different seasons of your life. That's normal.

1. The Body as First Language

Your body notices before your mind explains.

Tension, ease, fatigue, breath, ache, and relief are information, not inconveniences.

2. Pace Over Performance

Healing does not move faster because you demand it.

It moves when the nervous system feels safe enough to continue.

3. Boundaries as Care

Limits are not punishment.

They are how trust is protected.

4. Rest as Integration

Rest is not a pause from the work.

It is where the work lands.

5. Curiosity Over Certainty

Questions are not failure.

They are often the first sign of trust.

6. Choice Over Compulsion

You are no longer required to repeat what once kept you safe.

Awareness creates options.

7. Return Is Always Available

There is no falling off the path.

Only moments when you notice you've drifted and come back.

You do not need to embody all seven at once.

Integration is not symmetrical.

Appendix C: Optional Depth Work

The Wound. The Lesson. The Becoming.

A tarot-based, intuitive reflection practice

This appendix expands on the Optional Depth Work practice introduced earlier, offering a reference you can return to when needed.

This practice is optional.
It is not required for healing, growth, or completion of this workbook.

If tarot is not part of your language, you may skip this section entirely or adapt it using symbols, intuition, or free writing instead.

The Spread

You may use one card for each position, or reflect intuitively without cards.

- The Wound

  What shaped me. What hurt. What still pulls at the thread.

- The Lesson

  What I learned. What I survived. What I understand now.

- The Becoming

  What is emerging. What I am growing into. What is ready to live differently.

How to Use This Practice

Pull the cards slowly, or sit with the prompts without cards.

Ask:

- What is this showing me about where I've been?

- What wisdom is already integrated?

- What wants my attention now, gently?

You do not need to interpret perfectly.

You do not need to reach a conclusion.

This practice is about listening, not proving.

Return to this practice only when something asks. Leave it when it quiets.

Appendix D: Integration Maps

A visual way to notice patterns

This appendix expands on the Integration Maps practice introduced earlier, offering visual entry points you can return to when words feel heavy.

On a blank page, you might:

- Draw a spiral showing how themes return differently over time

- Sketch symbols for what steadies you

- Create a simple map of what you release, what you carry, what you protect

There is no right format.

This is about recognition, not artistry.

Lastly: Permission to Use This Your Way

This workbook is not linear.

Neither is healing.

You may return to one breath-poem for months and ignore the rest.

You may never open the tarot section.

You may write only in the margins.

All of that counts.

These pages exist so you don't have to search for what already steadies you.

Nothing here expires.

About the Author

Rowena Sowders is the author of *The Seeker's Lessons* and creator of *The Seeker's Workbook*, a companion for healing, integration, and becoming. A former mental health therapist with a master's in counseling, she brings a trauma-informed, body-aware lens to this work, grounded in lived experience rather than perfection.

Her approach weaves together psychology, intuitive practice, dreamwork, and the quiet wisdom of tarot. It honors both the clinical and the mystical without asking the reader to choose between them. She writes for those who have done the work of surviving and are learning how to live with what they now know.

Rowena believes healing is not a destination but a relationship, one built through presence, honesty, and the willingness to listen inward. Her work invites seekers to trust their own knowing, move at the pace of their bodies, and carry forward what truly holds.

She lives in the American Southeast with her husband and son, surrounded by books, yarn, well-loved mugs, tarot decks, and the steady magic of ordinary days.

Wherever you are in your story,
may you keep choosing softness over silence,
and curiosity over fear.
You were never lost.
You were always becoming.
Thank you for doing this work,
and for letting me walk beside you.

QUIET CUP
PRESS

www.ingramcontent.com/pod-product-compliance
Lightning Source LLC
Chambersburg PA
CBHW041536120626
46551CB00019B/2717